Rental Property Investing

How New Investors Can Dominate In Rental Properties

Money Grind Academy

The contents of this book may not be reproduced, duplicated or transmitted without direct written permission from the author.

Under no circumstances will any legal responsibility or blame be held against the publisher for any reparation, damages, or monetary loss due to the information herein, either directly or indirectly.

Legal Notice:

This book is copyright protected. This is only for personal use. You cannot amend, distribute, sell, use, quote or paraphrase any part or the content within this book without the consent of the author.

Disclaimer Notice:

Please note the information contained within this document is for educational and entertainment purposes only. Every attempt has been made to provide accurate, up to date and reliable complete information. No warranties of any kind are expressed or implied. Readers acknowledge that the author is not engaging in the rendering of legal, financial, medical or professional advice. The content of this book has been derived from various sources. Please consult a licensed professional before attempting any techniques outlined in this book.

By reading this document, the reader agrees that under no circumstances are is the author responsible for any losses, direct or indirect, which are incurred as a result of the use of information contained within this document, including, but not limited to, —errors, omissions, or inaccuracies.

© Copyright 2018 Dibbly Publishing.

All rights reserved.

Contents

INTRODUCTION 1

CHAPTER 1 WAYS TO COUNT THE RETURN ON YOUR MONEY 5
- DISCOUNTED CASH FLOW 9
- PRESENT VALUE 13
- TERMINAL VALUE 13
- RISK ADJUSTED RATE OF RETURN 15
- INTERNAL RATE OF RETURN 21

CHAPTER 2 WHAT NO ONE TOLD YOU ABOUT PROPERTY 27
- PURPOSE 30
- SURROUNDING LAND 32
- ACCESS 33
- FUTURE DEVELOPMENT 35
- ENVIRONMENTAL ISSUES 36

CHAPTER 3 HOW TO KEEP ON THE RIGHT SIDE OF THE LAW 39
- INDIVIDUAL STATUS 39
- LLC STRUCTURE 40
- C CORPORATIONS 43
- S CORPORATIONS 44
- STRUCTURING OWNERSHIP 44
- BALANCING STRATEGIES 47

CHAPTER 4 HOW TO GET BANKS AND LENDING INSTITUTIONS ON YOUR SIDE 51
- PREPARING BANK LOAN APPLICATIONS................................55
- RENTAL PROPERTY 56
- DON'T MAX OUT ON LOANS 58
- UNIMPROVED PROPERTY 59

CHAPTER 5 SECRETS YOU HAVEN'T HEARD ABOUT........63

CHAPTER 6 EAGLE EYE VIEW THAT COULD GIVE YOU THE EDGE 67
- THE CYCLES OF THE REAL ESTATE MARKET............................70
- TIMING THE MACRO CYCLES..71

CHAPTER 7 STRUCTURE REAL ESTATE INVESTMENT COMPANIES LIKE A PRO 73
- TAX CONSIDERATIONS..73
- OFFSHORE COMPANY SET-UP...76

CHAPTER 8 WAYS TO CUT LOSSES AND LET PROFITS RIDE 81

CONCLUSION..91

THANK YOU! 95

MORE BOOKS BY MONEY GRIND ACADEMY 97

Dibbly Publishing

Dibbly Publishing publishes books that inspire, motivate, and teach readers. Through lessons and knowledge.

Our Book Catalog

Visit https://dibblypublishing.com for our full catalog, new releases, and promotions.

Follow Us on Social Media

Facebook - @dibblypublishing

Twitter - @DibblyPublish

Download Your Bonus – Property Upgrades

Get all the support and guidance you need to be a success at getting the most from your property!

https://dibblypublishing.com/property-upgrades

Introduction

Real assets and financial assets have much in common. Real assets are things like land, building and structures, while financial assets are more like government bonds. This stream may have some variation to it, but it is, for the most part, a fairly stable stream. A typical US Government bond as a coupon perhaps, for illustration purposes, pays $3 for a $100 bond. That works out to be3%. That cash flow is fairly constant, and because the US Government is priced as risk-free, because it has never defaulted and holds AAA rating, you can be fairly confident that you will get that $3 payment every year on the dot.

That predictability is the benchmark for where you want to put your money. If you can earn 3% risk-free, then you know that all your other investments must be measured with that yardstick.

It is the same with real estate. If you can't get a risk-adjusted rate of return better than the US Treasury, then that investment is not something that you want to consider. We will look at this in greater detail later in the book, but your starting point should be to look at investments as a whole, and think about what your point of investing is.

Real estate is only one of the many possible avenues to make better, than average, returns on your capital. Each person's risk appetite, his outlook, and his financial ability are just a few of the factors that determine what investments in real estate are open to him.

As this book unfolds, we will look at how to evaluate the cash flow stream related to real estate and the rules of thumb that you can apply as you get into this, or as you advance your existing exposure in this exciting area of investing.

Once you understand the cash flow profile that you need to make this work, you can then start to look at the various components that add or detract from the value of a piece of property. Property is not limited to unimproved land. It can even include land with or without buildings. It can include just the building without the land, or it can include parts of the building. The best way to look at it is to look at the smallest unit that generates its own cash flow.

As an extension of that cash flow, you will need to look at the regulatory environment that surrounds your target property. Every obligation that needs to be discharged on that property is going to translate to some form of cost, and that, in turn, affects your cash flow and thus the price that you should be willing to pay for that property – so do your due diligence and get a good grip of the regulatory environment in that state and county you plan on making the purchase.

One secret to investing in real estate that most people are not aware of is the formula to perfectly leverage each and every investment. There is the perfect balance where you maximize your return just by the way you finance the property. Too much, and your risk goes up, thereby reducing the risk-adjusted returns. Too little, and you have invested too much equity and you will be left with reduced returns as well. To maximize your returns, you have to get the optimal leverage for your property. We will show you how in Chapter 4.

There are some tricks of the trade that you can employ, and we will go over them in the chapter after financing. By this point, you will already know about the secret of leveraging, and we will also reveal the secrets of structuring so that you could possibly reduce your risk with financial instruments and structural tricks. All the big boys are using them, its time you should too.

Once you get an understanding of all of this, we put in the finishing touches of the real estate investing process by showing you how to read the tea leaves when it comes to the macroeconomics of real estate, and even the underlying economy. This then dovetails into structuring your entire set-up so that you are shielded behind layers of corporate veils and offshore entities when possible. It is more for estate planning and risk aversion than anything else, but it can have a financial benefit if done right. As always, make sure you get proper advice from your lawyer and accountant.

With that overview, we are ready to get down to it.

Chapter 1

Ways to Count the Return on Your Money

Profits are a function of three factors, to put it simply. The first factor is the risk in getting that profit, and the second is the cost of the capital, or investment, that you had to put into it to get that profit; and the third is the opportunity cost of investing in that investment instead of something else. There are a number of other criteria that are important as well, but these are the first three you would look at when the investment is in the back-of-the-napkin stage.

To illustrate, imagine if you found ten bucks on the road in the middle of the desert, then that money has zero effort and zero cost in it and you could do just about anything with it without any concern about payback or cost. You would still want to get the most bang out of your good fortune, and you would look for the investment that returns the most to you. If you have ten opportunities, each would give you a different return for those ten bucks. You could lend it to Bob, who promises to give you $11 in a month – so you make a dollar in profit in a period of one month. Or you could purchase something at the store for ten bucks and sell it on eBay for $13 within a month. Or you could just spend it on candy and have a good time. The last one obviously has zero return and loss of capital. The second one has a return of $3 and the first one has a return of $1. Bob is certain to pay you back – you have no doubt, so that is a zero-risk investment and you get the full $1 for it, but the eBay sale is not a sure thing. You've seen the product sell before, but there are too many moving parts and too many variables. You think you can get it, but there is a risk. There is a risk that it doesn't sell and you're stuck with the product at worst case scenario, and the most you can make is $3 – that is the maximum upside potential.

So, which do you do?

It seems fairly obvious that you just lend Bob the money and be done with it. It seems like the best scenario possible. That's what unsophisticated investors will do.

So, does that mean that you go ahead and make the eBay investment? The one where you buy something and try to sell it online? Not necessarily. You need a significantly more sophisticated way of making the choice but, for now, the thing that you have to understand is that there are two dimensions when it comes to opportunity cost. You have the opportunity cost of making investments across various instruments. If you had ten bucks, you could purchase unimproved land, rental properties, and stocks in blue-chip companies, stocks in start-up companies, fixed income instruments and many more. The first layer you have to decide is which one you should invest in. In this book, we will not look at that layer of decision-making because it is assumed that you have already received the necessary professional guidance on how much to allocate to which asset class, and how much to allocate to real estate. That is your starting amount and so your second opportunity cost is which real estate opportunity to invest in.

There are numerous opportunities that your broker will show you, so you have to see which one gives you the best returns once they have been adjusted for risk. Adjusting for risk is more of an art than a science and, if you can properly understand that, then take the necessary steps to mitigate it and then ring-fence it with certain strategies. You will find that there is almost no instance of real estate investment that would be a loser.

This book will put you on that path and get you looking at the right factors, but the details are going to be too advanced for this level. We will cover that in another book.

There are five elements that you have to consider in each investment. They are the same, regardless if you are investing in real estate, or in bonds. The issue is the cash flow that comes from it over the course of time, and the terminal value that you think it will be worth at a certain point in the future. Since you have to compare apples to apples, you need to discount all that money back to the same point in time that you are making the investment, so the present time is the best possible period in time that you should anchor everything to. This is key. If you look at the purchase one year from today, then you should discount the cash flow to that date as well. If you look at the investments today, give or take 30days from the time you make the calculation to the time you plan on closing on the transaction, the idea is that the horizons should match.

Then there is the element of risk. Risk is not an unknown quantity as most people think it is. There is a stable default rate in most things. You just have to know what your investment's default rate of your purchase is. Your banker will typically know that. It's like your credit score. Your credit score is a numerical representation of the chances that you are going to default on your payments. It is your risk profile represented in a number. In the same way, you can look at what is called a risk premium in any form of financial asset. If you look at the REITs (Real Estate Investment Trusts) or ABS (Asset Backed Securities), you will see that they have various asset classes that are grouped together and they can mathematically predict the default rate of each asset class. That's what you want to do. You want to adjust your risk so that you get a good handle on what the return is going to be. It's just like knowing for certain the item on eBay (the example we started out with) is going to fare.

Getting a grip on these five elements would put you in good standing as far as looking intuitively and accurately at any potential investment.

Discounted Cash Flow

Discounted Cash Flow (DCF) has three components. To understand this, the first thing you need to do is look at the cash flow that is projected to occur over the life of the investment or the life of the asset. When you hear someone say that you need to discount something, you first think of a discount in price, like a sale or a bargain. In finance, that's not too far from the truth as well – the discount simply means to reduce the value from its original face value. So, if a bond has a face value of $1,000 and it matures in exactly one year, but you get to buy it today for $900, that means that you get a 10% discount. That's one way to look at it. The other way to look at it would be to see that you are investing $900 and getting a $100 return in one year. That means your yield is 100/900 which is 11.11%. If you are purchasing a US Treasury instrument, the chances are very low (next to none) that there will be no default, so you can pretty much count this as risk-free. There are a few things that you should extract from this example. The first is that you should use the risk-free rate as a guide to what you should expect to make for the investment. If you purchase a piece of property that is yielding less than your risk-free rate, than you know that it is not the best thing in the world that you should be investing in. Move on.

Coming back to DCF, the idea here is to discount the cash flow so that the stream of cash flows in the future is adjusted by the time value of money (and a couple of other factors which we will discuss a little later). For now, the idea is just to get comfortable with discounting the future cash flows to a point in the present so that we treat all the future cash flows in the same way.

To get the present value of a future payment, all you have to do is divide that payment by the discount rate plus 1 so, if you've determined that the risk-free rate is 11.11%, then, in decimal terms, 11.11% is 0.1111. All you have to do is divide it by 100. Once you get the decimal value, add that to 1, so now you get 1.1111. Divide the cash flow you will get one year down the road by this number so, if you are going to get $,1000 – the face value of the instrument, you take 1000/1.1111 and what you get is $900.

You may think that this just goes in one big circle and comes back to where we were in the beginning. Yes, it does – in this example. That was on purpose, so that you see how all the elements are related.

Typically, what you would do is use the discount rate to

see what the present value should be, and that would be the price you pay. When you discount the cash flow, the discount rate is a whole basket of factors. In this example, we only used one factor which is the time value of cash. We also just started the example over one period, in this case, that is one year, so the scenario here is that you put in 900 today, and one year later you receive $1,000 and that gives you the 11.11% yield.

Now, if that was made over a five-year period, then the logic is still the same, except you would have to compound the discounting factor for the number of years that it takes. Let's say in a fixed-income instrument, you expect that, at the end of the first year, you get $100 and the same at the end of the second, third, and fourth and, in the final year, you get the annual payment of $100 plus the repayment of the face value of $1,000. How much would you be willing to pay for the instrument assuming you need 11.11% yield?

Calculating that would be to simply discount the cash flow from each year and adding it up. In the first year, you would take 100/1.11 –that is straightforward and similar to the earlier example (earlier you took 1100 because the $1,000 face value was also returned at the same time the $100 was paid). In this example, the face value is not paid yet so you only need to discount the $100 – which is, in fixed income terminology, called the coupon payment, so discounting 100/1.11 gets you $90.10.

Then you go to the second year, and, because you need to compound the rate of return, you have to raise that discount rate to the power of 2 (because it is two years) so it will look like this – $100/(1.1111^2)$. In essence, you are dividing 100 by 1.2345 so you get $81. It's less than the $90.10 because, as you can imagine, there is a time value to cash, and the later you receive something, the less it is valued, so year two gets you $81.

In year three you do the same and divide the cash flow of $100 by 1.1111^3 since it's the third year. That means you get 100/1.3717, and that works out to $72.90. You do the same with the fourth year except you raise the denominator to the fourth power and you get $100/(1.1111^4)$ to get 100/1,5341 for a discounted value of $65.61.

In the final year, you have two events. That is, the payment of the coupon payment and the payment of the face value of $1,000. That means you have 1100 to be divided by 1.1111^5. That gives you 1.7045, so 1100/1.7045 is $645.

Now you add them all together to give you the maximum you should pay for that instrument with today's dollars - $649.57+$65.61+$72.9+$81+$90. That gives you $959.09 (there is some rounding error when calculated on the spreadsheet).

That last number, $959.09, should be the price you pay for an instrument that is going to pay you $100 every year and pay you $1,000 at the end of five years.

That is how DCF works. You can use it to see how much an asset is worth, based on the stream of cash it generates in a given period of time. You can take the same concept and apply it to real estate. As the chapter advances, we will show you how to do that.

Present Value

As in the last section, what you saw happen was that the future payments that you received were adjusted to reflect today's value according to a rate of return that takes into account the time value of funds. Have you noticed how lotteries and powerballs are paid out? If the winner wants, they will pay out the full state value, let's say 100 million, over the time agreed upon, which is usually ten years or more. The winner also has the option of taking it all today and, if they do that, they don't get the full 100 million as they get maybe 70 million. That is the present value of the total value in the future.

Terminal Value

The terminal value of any investment property or asset is a large factor in determining what you will be willing to put in the investment today. Take, for instance, that five year investment in the previous example. In that illustration, you put in $954 at the beginning and you received $100 every year. In the end, you got $1,000 on top of the annual $100 coupons, and those one thousand dollars in bond terminology is called the face value. In real estate, that is about the same thing as the point where you sell the property. If you think you are going to hold on to the property for ten years and collect rental income over that time, then sell it at the market value, then you would do the same sort of calculation that you would do with the example. The only difference is that you do not know what the terminal value is going to be.

Many people take a guess at what terminal values are going to be, and then they discount that back to make sure that there is sufficient profit potential in the discounted cash flow, or in the profit potential of the property.

The terminal value of any property can be controlled in a number of ways. These are the factors that can aid in your calculation of the terminal value of property:

1. Will improvements be made to the property?

2. Will the area around the property be developed?

3. Will the property be subjected to favorable economic factors? (See Chapter 6.)

These are typically positive effects on the property. If

you're buying a house in the area, one way to look at it would be to understand the local and state-wide plans for this area in which the property you are interested in is located. It would also be wise to talk to the local agents on what they think the future value of the property you are interested in would be.

The terminal value of your property is a major factor in your investment decision. It is something that you need to ascertain with calculated accuracy.

Risk Adjusted Rate of Return

To get to the core of this aspect of real estate investing, you need to have a good understanding of risk. The word 'risk' in finance carries a significantly different meaning from what we tend to hear when people talk about risk in general. In general, we see risk as a qualitative term that has no means of being calculated, other than just winging it by giving it your best guess. That's sufficient for kitchen table talk, but when it comes to real estate investments, you want to be able to quantify risk in a way that you can actually plug it into a simple equation and have it return a fairly accurate expression of the reality.

Risk is really just the standard deviation of an event outside its norm or expected event. There is a mathematical route to get to this number, but that would be way beyond the scope of this book. Suffice to say, risk is just the probability of the desired outcome not happening.

Analyzing risk and quantifying it takes a tremendous amount of experience and you should be able to get that as you develop your ability in real estate investments. Instead of using a quantitative method that is maths based, here is a simple, yet structured way, that you can adjust your discount rate. There are ten items that you need to score, and they are as follows:

1. Seller's Risk – This is the risk that you apply to the promoter of the project. It applies to different principals in different cases. If you are making a purchase from a developer, then this is a developer's risk. If you are making the purchase from an individual, then it is the risk associated with that person. The risk here is classified between 0 and 10, with 0 meaning there is no risk at all, and 10 meaning it is 100% risky. This means that there is a 100% certainty that your projections will falter because of the risks associated with the seller.

2. Debt Risk – In every real estate transaction, there is possibly a component of the purchase value that needs to be funded using some form of a debt instrument. That instrument could be a bank loan, or some other fixed income instrument. The risk here is dependent on three

factors. The first is the amount of leverage that is used to purchase the property. The higher the debt, the higher the cash flow is being levered and this presents a risk. The second is the codicils in the loan agreement, in particular if the interest rate is floating or fixed. A floating rate loan has the risk of the interest rate moving against it in time and that will change the cost structure of the property. Finally, there is the debt maturity risk. This is when there is a risk that a short-term loan on the property becomes due during a weak market, and the refinancing of the property comes at a rate that is unsustainable; a subsequent sale of the property could result in a loss and could trigger other issues as well.

3. Cash flow risk – Imagine if you are purchasing a property that is tenanted, then all that cash flow is related to whether your tenant pays their rent on time, remains in the unit for the duration of the contract (performance risk), and when they leave you have an immediate occupancy to continue the cash flow (roll over risk). Any variation from this is a hit to the cash flow and something that you should be protected against.

4. Tenant risk – In large tenanted properties where there are multiple tenants, there is a greater risk to occupancy concentrated with one or two clients. If you have a ten-floor building and all

ten floors are occupied by one tenant, then you run the risk of zero occupancy the moment that tenant moves. If you have five tenants in that building, then the risk that all five move out at the same time is less, and you have a lower risk of zero cash flow. You also have to evaluate the tenant based on his business's viability.

5. Natural Catastrophe – You have to evaluate the risk that you will face in the event there is a natural disaster that destroys the property, renders it uninhabitable, or otherwise disables it. There are certain catastrophes that can be mitigated with insurance, while there are others that cannot. You have to find the optimal insurance coverage to cover the basics, structure the assets in a certain way to manage the rest, and you eventually do have to take on some of the risk – as long as you are aware of it.

6. Liability – Owners of property have responsibility towards injury that occurred on the property, and you have to make sure that you are properly insulated from that liability overflowing the bounds of the insurance that you should have in place for it and flows over into other assets. You have to make sure that your assets are properly structured to the fullest extent of the law to make sure that you ring-fence the property tightly.

7. Political Risk – Just as with any investment, you have to be acutely aware of the political winds that blow from time to time because politics has implications on the regulatory framework and it has implications on the environment that the businesses in the area thrive on. Understand the political landscape that affects your property and, instead of backing out of investments for this reason, look at the way of protecting it by the appropriate structuring and risk protection strategies that are available.

8. Social risk – Each neighborhood that is host to the property being invested in is subject to a social change over time. That social change, which includes demographic change, population migration, as well as the fundamentals that support the property of that town, are all functions of the market value of the property that is being invested in. Take, for instance, a town that is employed mostly by a single conglomerate. If 60% of the population works for the company, and another 30% work in supporting industries, what you have is a high-risk situation that cannot be totally structured away. If the company cuts that operation or goes out of business, then all the town people lose their jobs and the market value in the area will plummet. You have to understand the town and the demographics that you are buying into. When

you look at property, you have to look at the social aspect of the revenue line.

9. Inadequate Operating Capital – As a property owner, it is your responsibility to conduct repairs and keep the functioning of the property in a good and safe order. You are also liable for what's under the ground (i.e. if someone buried radioactive material in the ground, it is your responsibility to get it cleaned up). That is, of course, an extreme example, but it drives the point that you need to have adequate reserves of cash, or a line of credit that can go to keeping the place running. You are also typically responsible for the operational aspects of the property. If you own rental property, then everything from the hot water to the kitchen sink needs to be in good operating condition, and you need to be able to have them fixed on time and without hesitation. A LACK of resources will render your property inoperable and possibly impact your cash flow stream.

10. Estate Planning – When you invest in property, you are probably doing it for the income and the capital appreciation potential of that property. In any case, these are long-lasting assets and you probably have a terminal point in the future in mind; however, you need to make sure that you have it structured in a way that takes into account

estate planning. Estate planning differs from state to state. If you have all your property in one state, that is complicated in its own right, but it gets significantly more complicated when you start owning property in different states. There are ways to structure this, and we will look at it later in the book.

All these factors have an impact on the rate of return that you should use, which would justify the investment. One thing to remember in all of this is that sophisticated property investors employ professional managers to look into these factors and analyze the exact risk that they face. Once they do that, they mitigate those risks, and the ones that can't be mitigated are ring-fenced away from the property, it's cash flow stream, and, more importantly, from the principal's other assets. You can build up to that level, but for those of you just starting out, while it may seem daunting, you have to do much of this on your own and get outsourced help when needed.

Internal Rate of Return

The Internal Rate of Return, or IRR, is an important aspect of the real estate investment world. It gives you the tools you need to compare the investment opportunities in a structured and organized manner. Before you can fully appreciate or apply the IRR, you need to understand NPV. Now, NPV does not have its own section because we have already covered the process of getting the NPV, but in a different context – DCF, or Discounted Cash Flow. The only thing that was missing in the DCF example was the amount of the present investment that mans the amount of money that was put into it. The NPV is a concept that you should understand because it takes into account all the money that goes in, and all the money that comes out. In DCF, we look at the cash that came in, whereas, in NPV, we take the DCF and superimpose the cash that goes out to pay for that asset as well.

If you are purchasing the property for cash, then your cash number is placed as a negative number upfront because the positive and negative numbers indicate outflow and inflow respectively.

If you intend to expend cash down the road for major improvements, then you should place negative flows in the appropriate time spots along the cash flow streams.

Once you have all the positive and negative numbers in place, then you are ready to sum them up. In the last example, your outlay was for $900 with $100 a year for the next five years and $1,000 payment. In present value terms, it would look like this:

Time	0	1	2	3	4	5	NPV
Cash Flow	$(900.00)	$100.00	$100.00	$100.00	$100.00	$1,100.00	
Discount Rate	11.11%	11.11%	11.11%	11.11%	11.11%	11.11%	
Discounted Cash Flow	$(900.00)	$90.00	$81.00	$72.90	$65.61	$649.57	$59.09

This doesn't mean that your profit is $54.21. It means it is above your required return of 11.11%. Remember we said that the price of the investment should be no more than $954.21, at 1.11% return, and now that you only invested $900, this means that you gained $54.21 above the required return. That is your NPV. How does this jive with the IRR? The IRR is the discount rate that you use to get a zero NPV.

In other words, the IRR is a percentage of return that brings this excess $54.21 down to zero. That means that you can alter the internal rate down to a point (in this case, less than 11.11%). It is not easy to calculate the number that will result in the zero, but a spreadsheet program can easily handle it if you use the Goal Seek Function. This is what that would look like:

Time	0	1	2	3	4	5	NPV
Cash Flow	$(900.00)	$100.00	$100.00	$100.00	$100.00	$1,100.00	
Discount Rate	12.83%	12.83%	12.83%	12.83%	12.83%	12.83%	
Discounted Cash Flow	$(900.00)	$88.63	$78.55	$69.62	$61.70	$601.51	$0.00

The program solves for a discount rate which would result in the NPV being zero, and you will see in this spreadsheet an excerpt that the discount rate of 12.83% is needed to make the NPV zero. That essentially means that the investments are using a 12.83% return to model its profile. If you compare each investment by their IRR, you start to see the one that has the best return in the highest discount rate. If they all have the same discount rate, you see the one with the highest NPV.

Let's just look at this one more time. The DCF, NPV, IRR and terminal value give you a good place to start your comparison of all the various real estate opportunities that you may have. When you compare all the same investments in a particular class, then you set the discount rate identically for all of them. Now, look at the NPV. You can rank the investment according to NPV.

If you look at your required rate of return as your benchmark, then set all the investments to zero NPV and compare them by the resulting IRR. This gives you two ways to qualitatively compare all the investments that you have in front of you.

As a reminder before we close out this chapter, I want to highlight an important point that you may have not considered. While it is in your best interest to mitigate as much risk as possible in the pursuance of an investment, it is also worth noting that return is a function of risk. The lesser return you are willing to take, the less profit you will extract from the investment structure. If you were to cordon off and appropriate all the various risk factors to external sources (third party sources), then you are, in essence, bringing yourself back to just taking on the risk-free rate of return.

Chapter 2

What No One Told You About Property

There is a lot that happens behind the scenes with sophisticated investors in property that the individual investors don't really know about. These are not illegal in any way but require savvy and risk-averse professionals who understand the market that they play in, and understand the financial instruments that are available to them.

What no one tells you about property is that you have to take an active position in the property to be able to make larger profits, instead of passive positions that see you make close to risk-free rates. If you are going to only make a risk-free return on the property, you might as well just invest in T-Bills and save yourself from the headache that comes attached to any real estate investment.

When you look at the property you want to purchase, this is the framework you need to work within so that it iteratively looks at what you want out of it, and looks at the elements of the investment. When you go back and forth with it, you will eventually come to the final profile of your investment. You need to have purpose instead of emotion, reason instead of intuition, and the big picture instead of only short-sighted factors when coming to a decision to make an investment.

Real estate investment is not about getting cozy with the idea of owning lots of land across the country; real estate investment is like any investment in that its sole purpose is for you to be able to grow your money. That growth has to either keep your money at the same purchasing power in the future as it has now, or it has to be able to grow your money so that you have more tomorrow than you have today, beyond its rate of inflation.

If you want to become wealthy and wealth creation is your purpose of investing, then you need to take on a larger risk profile because only risk can return you a super natural profit profile. Think about that for a minute.

A point to note about inflation. If you have a dollar today, and that dollar can buy you an egg sandwich, you want to be able to purchase the same egg sandwich next year with a dollar that you put away, but that egg sandwich is going to cost you $1.04 next year because of the natural rise in all kinds of demand and costs. That natural rate is the inflation rate and, in the US, that rate is between 2 and 4%. In 2017, that was about 2.1% so if you bought that egg sandwich in 2016 for $1, in 2017, that same egg sandwich would be priced at $1.02. If you put a dollar under your pillow in 2016 and hoped to take it out in 2017 to buy the same egg sandwich, you would not be able to because the vendor would now be asking for a slightly higher value. That is inflation.

The purpose of your investment is, at the very least, to be able to have the money that you have saved to keep up with inflation so that you can buy the same thing next year with the money that you saved this year. If you want to have the same purchasing power with your cash, you need to invest it in a way that will give you, at least the same return, as the rate of inflation. If you stuck that money in a risk-free investment that returned 2.1%, then you will be able to have $1.02 next year and that will allow you to purchase that favorite egg sandwich of yours.

Let's be clear about one thing – this is not going to make you wealthy – this just keeps your money at par with the rate of inflation. Becoming wealthy is about being paid for your efforts and so you need to put in effort in one of different ways. If you are going to start a business, that's one way to put in the effort. If you are not, then you need to be able to stomach the risk and, by taking on that risk, you will be able to create wealth.

The bottom line is that investing to sustain savings is very different from investing to create wealth. You need to know exactly what you are aiming for when you set yourself on a path to investment.

The reason property is so popular is because it is taken for granted that property prices, for the asset's market value, will rise with the tides. That means you don't have to worry about the state of anything else. As long as you can keep the payments up, you will be able to reap the profits in the end when you sell the property for a higher price. This is a dangerous strategy and it was the root cause of the 2008 economic meltdown.

Ideally, you should be able to invest in the property and take the risk that it presents, mitigating it wherever possible, and taking on the rest so that you can gain the opportunity at wealth creation. If you are looking to create wealth, then you mitigate the foreseeable risk and absorb the unforeseeable one and that leaves you with the right purpose.

Purpose

Purpose defines your intentions. As you saw at the top of the chapter, if you intend on preserving purchasing power, then your purpose in investing is different from a person whose intention is wealth creation. If you have both intentions, then that creates a different basket of investments. Your objective is to not confuse the two intentions and to keep your investment basket isolated from each other so that you can keep the risk profiles separate.

If you structure your investment basket according to

purpose, and then further, by asset class, you will find that they are easier to manage and make more sense than if you arrange them based on purely asset classes. Your purpose would determine the discount rate to use and that would determine the asset to invest in. For instance, if your purpose was to sustain purchasing power, then you would only need to have an IRR of 2.1%, and any investment that gives you that or exceeds that would be within your scope.

That is economic purpose.

You also want to understand the purpose of the land. Is it agricultural land, is it commercial, residential or whatever the designation may be. You need to understand what the regulation around that land is, and what you are allowed to do with it. You need to understand the limitation of the land and/or asset. For instance, if you see this large piece of land that you intend on converting to a factory, you need to understand the zoning laws in the county and what you are able to do with it or otherwise.

When you invest in an asset, do the following:

1. Check with the county on the history of the ownership and what has been done on that property for the last 30 – 50 years.

2. Find out the history of the asset (i.e. legal claims, issues, liabilities, and former use).

3. Ascertain the future plans of the county and how the land will be treated in the near future.

Surrounding Land

It is not sufficient that you look at the land that you are interested in investing. You need to look at the land that surrounds it, or the assets that surround your proposed purchase. If you plan on investing in undeveloped land, then you need to understand what that land has potential for. That potential is determined and dependent upon what is surrounding it. Many real estate investments include the purchase of land and then the building of an apartment complex on that land. If the neighboring land was empty at the time of purchase of your land and, after you had committed to the purchase you find that the neighboring land was to become a factory or a barn yard (again depending on the zoning), you will find that you will have a big hurdle to overcome in terms of getting rental income from the apartment building. This is a simple example, but it is there to highlight the issue of understanding exactly what you need to do to make sure that your purchase gives you the return you plan on over the time horizon that you are looking at.

Access

Accessing your property is an important aspect of the price in the future and the income that you can derive from over the course of ownership. You must understand the physical access profile of your investment property and the kind of access that you are allowed. You will be surprised with the number of complications that arise because the property one purchases is offset from the main road and requires permission of the intermediate property owner to get across.

Make sure that you negotiate the access you want to the property you are purchasing before you sign up for the purchase. Once you make the purchase, the negotiating advantage lies with the property owner you need to negotiate with. If you haven't signed up, you can negotiate a contingency agreement and that would not be as expensive a proposition as if you have already bought the property and are now forced to deal with the consequences.

It is naive to think that just because you purchase a property that you will automatically be given access to it by your neighboring land owners. That is never the case. You have to negotiate this access ahead of time and the best way this can work for you is if you negotiate the sale price down with the seller for this reason, but, at the same time, negotiate the easement with the neighbor.

Remember the land owners that surround you are in no way bound to provide you with access to your land. For all they care, you could helicopter in to your land. In fact, it can be considered trespass to cross their land to get to yours if they tell you so explicitly.

There are three issues that you need to consider when it comes to access:

1. Is there public access that you can connect to without encroaching on private property?

2. Is the access relevant and able to handle the traffic you foresee for the asset you are intending on purchasing?

3. If landlocked, are any of the surrounding owners willing to sell you the rights to easement before you purchase the landlocked land?

In the third scenario, remember that easement is a significant issue and often used as a negotiating strategy. There are landlocked assets that are forced to sell at a discount to their neighbors because they are unable to do anything with their land since there is no proper access. If you are unable to get a pre-negotiated agreement settled before the purchase, do not move forward because the price of the easement will go up after you have bought the landlocked property.

One strategy that I have seen work for real estate investors is to pursue owners of landlocked properties and then reach out to those who may be willing to liquidate their position at a substantial discount to market value. This would be doable if, and only if, you would be able to negotiate with the owners of the adjacent properties to allow an easement, or if you would be willing to buy the land that sits between you and the closest public access.

Good investments are not always just the plain vanilla ones that you see in the classified sections. You can make a hefty return if you are willing to do some extra work, like buying out two pieces of land and giving the landlocked property access.

Future Development

The future development of the area in which you plan in investing in is an important consideration. It does not mean that you must only purchase assets that are sitting in the middle of robust development, and it also does not mean that you must purchase assets that have no development slated for the area. The key is to look at property that is relevant to the plans you have in mind.

If you plan on purchasing the property to build bungalows and the land around your area is looking to build storage units, then you are going to have a bit of a problem. Some bungalow developers purchase the land surrounding the high-end development and either leave it empty or manicure it into a park so as to keep the bungalow property priced well. It creates a bit of a buffer zone.

The best way to get a feel for future development is to do a thorough due diligence of the town and county and to hire a real estate lawyer to do the investigation at the county clerk's office about future development in the area.

Environmental Issues

Environmental issues are probably furthest from your mind, but make sure that you change that right now. Any environmental issues that plagued the property before could become your headache after it is purchased. You should check with the EPA or, and with, the state environmental offices if the land or the surrounding area is facing, or will potentially face, environmental concerns.

When it comes to land and property assets, the urgency and critical nature of environmental issues is significant. If you do not do your EPA study and proceed with something that you think is irrelevant, it could come back later and force you to undertake corrective measures that would cost you and alter your returns from what you have projected. That would be the least of your worries if it stopped there, but it may not and may actually compound into penalties and fines due to non-compliance. The environmental due diligence is the owner's responsibility and ignorance is not a defense so make sure you get a lawyer that is adept at investigating these matters.

So, as a recap, here are five things that you need to add to the things that everyone has already told you. The first is that you need to make an absolutely clear distinction in your mind on the purpose of your purchase. You need to understand what your investment purpose is, and you need to understand what the asset's purpose is. The next thing you need to understand is the nature and status of the surrounding properties. You have to understand what your neighbors do, and who they are, and then you need to use common sense to see if your asset is going to perform in the way you intend it to perform under those circumstances.

You then need to look at access and easements. You never take access to your property for granted. If you purchase a landlocked property, you have to make sure that you have some form of an agreement with the neighboring owner before you finalize on the landlocked property; otherwise, it will work against you. You also need to look at the prospect of future development, and how it impacts your plans while you remain as owner. This is especially poignant if you are improving the property for a better terminal value.

Chapter 3

How to Keep on the Right Side of the Law

There are a number of ways that you could take ownership of a piece of property. For one, you could just walk out and buy the property under your own name – as you would your primary home. There is nothing wrong with that and you could even rent that property out and collect an income from that which will be reported on your Schedule E. There are no issues that you need to worry about and it is the simplest way to go about purchasing property.

Individual Status

The best thing about purchasing a property under your own name is that it is simple. There are no extra legal fees incurred in setting up the companies, and there is no need to do annual accounts and incur costs there. Overall, purchasing the property under your own name is easy, cost-effective and fast – as long as everything stays according to plan.

The downside is that this investment property could incur liabilities. For instance, the owner could get sued for some form of injury and the spillover of issue could flow into the other areas of the individual's life. It is never a good idea for you to take on a complex real estate transaction under your own name.

If you are just buying a single rental property home and you want to rent it out, then that is not so much of a problem. In fact, you will be able to get insurance to take on the liability in such a way that your personal assets are ring-fenced and they are not harmed in the event of a lawsuit, but anything more than a simple rental property would deserve to have its own LLC as part of the ownership structure and we will look at that next.

LLC Structure

This kind of company is extremely popular and, because of that, its filing fees are typically higher in most states. There are a few states that have lower prices, but those may not be optimal for real estate purposes. You are better off looking at something within your own state, or checking with your attorney or accountant who is familiar with your situation. The cost that you would incur annually for an LLC is as follows:

Kentucky LLC	$40
Arizona LLC	$50
Arkansas LLC	$50
Colorado LLC	$50
Hawaii LLC	$50
Iowa LLC	$50
Michigan LLC	$50
Mississippi LLC	$50
New Mexico LLC	$50
California LLC	$70
Montana LLC	$70
Utah LLC	$70
Nevada LLC	$75
Delaware LLC	$90
Indiana LLC	$90
Ohio LLC	$99
Georgia LLC	$100
Idaho LLC	$100
Louisiana LLC	$100
Maryland LLC	$100
New Hampshire LLC	$100
Oklahoma LLC	$100
Oregon LLC	$100
Virginia LLC	$100
West Virginia LLC	$100
Wyoming LLC	$100
Missouri LLC	$105
Nebraska LLC	$105
South Carolina LLC	$110
Florida LLC	$125

New Jersey LLC	$125
North Carolina LLC	$125
Pennsylvania LLC	$125
Vermont LLC	$125
Wisconsin LLC	$130
North Dakota LLC	$135
Rhode Island LLC	$150
South Dakota LLC	$150
Connecticut LLC	$160
Minnesota LLC	$160
Kansas LLC	$165
Maine LLC	$175
Washington LLC	$180
Alabama LLC	$183
New York LLC	$200
Washington D.C. LLC	$220
Alaska LLC	$250
Tennessee LLC	$300
Texas LLC	$300
Massachusetts LLC	$500
Illinois LLC	$150

The benefit of this company structure is that you can carry losses or profits directly onto your income tax and treat them as your losses or your income. It makes things simple and, at the same time, it helps to limit liability to within the corporate structure. More importantly, it is the best structure to have when you are pooling your resources to include a number of people who are putting their money together. There is no limit to the number of shareholders of an LLC, but, if you are purchasing this for yourself, there is not much benefit other than the profit/loss flow through – and, in some cases, that is not entirely desirable.

C Corporations

Another possible set-up you could look at is the C Corp. C Corps are the companies that you always hear about, they are legal entities and have rights and obligations. They pay taxes on their income and have a board of directors to oversee them. They are distinctly separate from their owners, and any income that is derived by their operations are considered the company's income and do not flow through to you. It's just like buying shares in a company. If you bought Apple shares, you are not liable for their taxes. There is a clear firewall between you and the company and its operations.

The problem here though is that you would pay income tax twice. The first time you would pay tax at the corporate level, and the second time is when the dividends are directed to the shareholders as you would have to pay taxes again by declaring those dividends as income. Savvy investors do not take the investments out and plow it back into the company, either taking in more assets or eventually selling the company and taking the profit as capital gains.

S Corporations

S Corps and LLCs have a lot of similarities in the way income and dividends are passed through to the owners. The only obvious difference is that S Corps and LLCs have a different number of maximum shareholders. S Corps have a limit of 100 shareholders, while LLCs have no minimum. If you are setting up a company for yourself and your family, then the difference doesn't really matter and the choice will most likely fall to the cost of incorporation, filing and annual fees.

Structuring Ownership

Why do we need to structure ownership of assets – not just real estate? There are two reasons why. The first is to separate the asset and the second is to shield ourselves. When you separate the asset from our personal asset, it not only makes managing it easy, it also removes prying eyes from knowing what we own. That may seem like a funny way of going about life, especially when we see transparency in all we do, but we keep our business ventures private so that we can keep our private lives secure. Having large ownership stakes under our personal name tends to attract nuisance suits. Nuisance suits can sometimes penetrate and become a real problem, but even if they don't, it costs us time and money to dispose of.

To avoid all of this, it is best to keep all our investment properties carved out and protected in corporate structures.

My suggestion is that you set up three tiers in the structure. The first tier is a C Corporation. This company operates independently of you and does not need to carry your name in the list of officers. You can set it up in such a way that you have professional administrators manage and administer the company under a trust agreement. This company's first layer of defense is that you are not part of the Board of Directors or the management of the company and so the assets held here will not be related back to you. However, if someone decides to penetrate this company with a little more digging, they will be able to find the list of shareholders.

The thing here is that finding shareholders' names can happen in two ways. This can happen by a person interested in knowing the ownership structure of a property does some digging, or the person who is interested in knowing your background does some digging. When you protect your assets, you have to look for ways to protect both paths to revelation.

The second thing you have to do is balance your needs with the cost and the complexities involved in setting up layers of corporations. In my experience, the basic structure that will serve the purpose and remain optimally cost efficient is to have a four-tiered structure.

This four-tiered structure will contain LLCs to own the property. This is the first layer. Each property you own should be held under this structure so A Corp will own property A, B Corp will own Property B, and so on. This is Tier D – the lowest in the hierarchy of the ownership tiers. These LLCs will typically be formed in the state the asset is located, so an apartment building in Wichita, KS will be placed in an LLC registered in Kansas.

The second last tier LLC (Tier C LLC) will hold a number of Tier D LLCs and they will do so according to a predetermined formula. To determine this formula, you need to understand the financial purpose of the asset. For instance, if the asset is to collect a stable rental income, then you place a bunch of LLCs from Tier D with stable rental incomes together. Tier D LLCs will have their income flow through and land in the Tier C LLC.

Tier B set-ups have a slightly different purpose. Here the companies hold assets that have the primary purpose of capital gain. That means you plan on selling those properties in the next five to ten years. Tier B companies are typically S Corps and the assets are left in them and the earnings are used to pay the loans associated with them, with the company holding on to those assets (each asset in this company is also held by a Tier D LLC).

Finally, you have the Tier A S Corp. This company is ideally set up in a state that protects shareholder identity. This Tier A company will wholly own Tier B and Tier C companies (remember B and C own Tier D companies).

There are other kinds of assets that you could acquire under this strategy; this could include real estate for the purpose of logging timber, development, rental property, agricultural land, parking structures, and so on.

You also should take into consideration succession issues. If you plan on leaving these assets behind, you should consult your estate planners about how to handle estate planning as well. Typically, the assets are placed in a trust and the trust continues to pay out to whomever it is instructed to do, so that would normally take care of the estate planning issues.

Balancing Strategies

It is not necessary to pool all the companies by the assets they own. In other words, you don't need to put all the rental properties in one, and all the development properties in another. You do not need to pool them by expertise because you are not actually having companies managed by full-time employees to benefit from economies of the learning curve. Instead, you are putting them together purely for the financial accounting of the assets.

So, let's say, for instance, you put together stable rental properties in one basket and that income flows through to the parent company. You could use that positive cash flow to secure financing for another property that is not entirely cash flow positive but you know that in five years you will be able to reap a healthy appreciation in its asset price.

This way, the loss of income on the asset appreciation property will offset taxable income from the revenue earning property while the cash flow is used to finance it. When the time comes, the entire group of assets could be sold and the gain in asset value will be treated as capital gains.

It is a simple strategy and these strategies can get more involved and more complex depending on the mix of assets that you take on, but the point is to shine the light on the four-tier system that you can use to move things around the table.

What you do not want to do is open yourself to nuisance lawsuits, or sacrifice the bulk of the assets by relating it to a failing asset, or an asset that is part of a law suit. The idea is to be able to extract profits as a pool and use it to fund other assets but, at the same time, to cut it loose without affecting the other properties if it loses money beyond what is beneficial or gets sued for damages. The option to eject any specific property at will is priceless if you structure it well.

One other thing that structuring will teach you is that the business of buying, selling, and investing in property is not one that is random or whimsical. It is a highly structured and disciplined business.

Chapter 4

How to Get Banks and Lending Institutions on Your Side

The first thing that you have to consider when you embark on real estate investment is that you have a strong credit rating. If your credit rating is poor, then you need to fix it and come back to the market once you have a strong rating.

The reason for this is that the stronger your credit rating, the cheaper your loans are going to be and the more you will be able to get in terms of loans. Ideally, you should not have any credit card debt or car loans, and you should have a property loan that you service without any delinquency.

The second thing that you should know is that you need to have a good relationship with a bank that is friendly to real estate investments. A bank that understands your credit history and is willing to look at your real estate deals will be in a good position to assist you with a loan for the properties that you take on.

Most people think that they can just apply for the full price of the property and service the payments with the income of the property. What they do not understand is that banks keep rebalancing their portfolios and they have the right to call the loan if they decide that it is a poor risk – one of the ways it classifies as a poor risk is:

1. If it is highly levered, and

2. If there are uncertain payment streams (meaning you've missed payments frequently in the past or are constantly 30 days behind).

Your key strategy is to never have the property over-levered.

For this reason, you should only take up a loan that is 70% of the most conservative estimate. Don't base the loan on the purchase price (the bank will do that) but for your own threshold and decision-making. To mitigate the risk of having your loan foreclosed, take the following steps:

1. Never make late payments.

2. Use the lowest of valuations in your analysis and then apply for a loan that is no more than 60% of the value of the property valuation.

3. Collateralize the loan adequately and, if possible,

it will be alright to slightly over-collateralize it so that there is no risk (comparatively speaking) for the bank.

A good rule of thumb to seek bank loans, regardless if they want to lend you more is to look at the amount of revenue you will generate from that property. If your property is going to generate $3,000 in monthly revenue, then take two-thirds of that and find a loan that has a fixed rate mortgage over the longest period possible. Let's say that you take a loan out for 30 years with a repayment of $2,000 per month. The maximum you will be able to borrow is approximately two hundred times more than the repayment you are willing to make. So, if you are looking to only pay $2,000 per month while you receive $3,000, and you plan on borrowing that for 30 years, then you could take on a loan for $400,000. This means that if you are going to buy a property with a 60% leverage, you divide 400,000 by 0.6. The value of the property that you can then look for is $666,667. You would then have to put in a down payment of $267,667 for this property.

As far as the bank is concerned, they have an asset that is 1.67 x their loan exposure and they have a repayment that is only two-thirds of the revenue that is being generated. The bank will feel safe with this.

The bank would also gain further comfort if you collateralize the loan by making sure that all income is channeled to the account that services the loan and the bank has first access to those funds for the monthly repayment. You should also place an automatic payment instruction at the time of the loan payment every month. Once you reach $12,000 in reserves (which you will reach if you do not touch the rental money that comes in every month), then you can start paying off the loan at a faster rate. Instead of paying $2,000 per month, you can start paying off $3,000 per month. If you have nothing else better to do with the funds, re-invest it. Whatever happens, try to not splurge with that extra income. If you can't re-invest it, at least expedite the repayment of the loan, or use it to make another purchase.

If you are going to do this, make sure that your loan does not have a prepayment penalty or if it does, make sure you understand when that lock-in period for prepayment ends.

This is a good way to ratchet up your holdings.

Loans are a funny thing. It feels like a good way to get your foot in the door, but, in the long run, the more you borrow, the less you make because interest, over time, is a major drain on your income. For instance, the loan in the example above was calculated with a 4.5% annual rate. Over the course of 30 years, you would have paid more than $320,000 in interest payments. If you increase your payments to $3,000, that is one thousand more every month that will go towards reducing the interest payments and, subsequently, the principal amount by a considerable margin.

Don't just repay the loan whenever you can, you also have to compare it to see if you can use the cash to take on another property and assist with the loan payments for that property as well.

The rationale behind property investment is different if you are looking for income on a monthly basis. If you want to supplement your income (and this is so for older investors), then what you want to do is use the extra income every month for your own living. If you are looking to create wealth, then you should re-invest that extra cash so that you can take on another property. If you combine the two properties and look at their cash flows and their terminal asset value, this will give you a good idea of how much your net worth will increase to by the time the loan ends. This means that if you are 30 today, and the loan is for 30 years, you can expect the property to be worth five times what it is now. Your $266,667 investment today and diligent payments from your tenant will result in a $3 million property when you retire. That's just one asset. What about if you multiply this a few times? The wealth starts to add up.

Preparing Bank Loan Applications

Preparing a loan application is not that difficult. You just need to have a narrative and the documents you have should fit that narrative and you should supplement that with a strong credit rating for yourself and limited current liabilities. If you have that, the bank is going to want to lend you the money. In fact, if anything, you should take less than what the banks offers you, not the other way around.

Make sure you do not fall for the trick where the bank gives you a super low starter rate and then ratchet it up later to a higher amount and lock you in. If you have the choice between a lock-in period and having to choose a fixed loan, take the fixed loan if it costs less. It is always better to pay a little more for certainty, than to pay less for uncertainty.

Rental Property

There is more than one way to structure rental properties and you should make it a point to have the necessary due diligence at your fingertips. That includes the market price for rental for the neighborhood you are buying into. The current renter's occupancy agreement will go a long way if you can keep them on. You should also have photographs of the property, and photographs of the properties in the neighborhood. If your bank is local, they will know the property well, or if they have a branch in that area, you will be able to call into their branch for an idea. What you should do is have it appraised by three different accredited appraisers, and then submit all three appraisals to the bank, but, in the calculation, make sure you use the lowest one. That tells the bank that you are conservative, and they are safe. If you can get a list of property values over the course of the last ten years, then that will go a long way as well because it shows how well the property has fared over time.

When you have the property evaluated, make sure that you tell the contractor to make a note of all the items that need replacement in the next year, two years, three years, four years and five years.

When you get this, convert it into a cash flow so that you know what your budget would be five years into the future. This applies to any investment property that you are purchasing when there is a home or an apartment block or even office space. You have to have an expert lay out your future expenses so that you can prepare for them and even have the current owner replace some of the items that need to be replaced in the next one year. Typically, heating, ventilation and AC systems, roofing and insulation, water pipes and such should be looked at and mapped out for repayment. All these need to be included in the cash flow projections so that you get a detailed look at your ability to withstand stresses on the cash flow.

Don't Max Out on Loans

It is very tempting to take on higher loans and let the winds blow where they may, but this is never a good idea, even if the banks are willing to lend them to you. We all saw how that worked out in the last economic crash. You have to be the one that decides how much and what you can afford in the worst of situations and, if you can do that, then the rest is just a waiting (until the property matures) game.

The temptation to take on full loans and max out the rental income on payments is never a good idea because landlords have responsibilities and they have duties to the tenant and those using the property. If you max out the loan based on the rental income, then there are two hazards waiting for you around the corner. The first is that there is a risk that the tenant misses a rental or is late – which means you have to cover the bank payment or else your loan gets flagged. The second is that he misses the payment altogether and you are now left holding the obligation. There is also the risk that he moves out and, while you refurbish the place and clean it up, you will be running in the red with no revenue. Those who do not foresee this end up having to put this on their credit card and the cost of that is significantly more than you can imagine. Cash advances or overdrafts cost money – more than the opportunity cost for keeping a running balance as a buffer and as operating costs for unintended repairs and forecasted maintenance.

Unimproved Property

If you happen to be purchasing property that has not been developed and you plan on developing it yourself, then there is a good chance that you would want to set it up a little differently than what we discussed in the section 'Structuring Ownership' found in Chapter 3.

That structure was primarily meant for assets that are already generating a cash stream. If your initial purchase is not the only major cash outflow, then you need to look at it as a property that needs development and, for that, you need to set aside funds above and beyond what is needed for the purchase of the asset.

There is the possibility for a home equity loan, but that comes back to what we said earlier and it should not be considered. There are two ways you can do unimproved financing.

The first way is to take a loan on 40% of the value of the asset, and, as long as you have good credit, the bank is going to go for it because they know that if you default there is more than enough equity in the land to get a payback, but be prepared that this loan is going to be expensive. Then set up a development company, separate from the asset-owning company, and make that a C Corp where you can have as many shareholders as you like and you can invite other investors to put in the equity needed to develop the property.

So, let's say you purchase a plot of land that plot of land is financed to the tune of 40% of the market value. Your cash investment into this so far is 60% of the market value. The development company that has been open to equity investors then contracts with the land owner and pays it a deposit to begin development. In return for the land, the developer gives the land owner 40% of the profits, while it keeps 60%. The Gross Development Value of the property should be no less than 4x the market price of the land. This means that the development company can pay a monthly progress payment that will eventually be deducted from the 40% value.

This should be enough to cover the monthly payments on the land. So, at this point, the investor is only out the 60% of the unimproved market value of the land. Once the development is complete and the properties are sold at 4x property value, the land owner gets 40% of that minus the monthly progress payments he has been receiving. In essence that 1.6x his property value. Paying back the loan and the interest incurred, should still leave him with 1.15x of the property value. His original investment was 0.6x of the property value and his return is 1.15x the property value. That means he made a 91% return on his property investment over 3 years. But that's not all, there is still the development side of the equation.

The cost of the development would be approximately 1x the property value and the land was 1.6x. That's a total of 2.6x land value. The remaining 1.4x after costs would work out to be about 1.3x land value. The original promoter of the project typically would hold 51% of the company and that would mean 0.637x property value will be divided by the equity participants who invested the 1x property value as costs for the construction (not taking into account anything here was financed by debt). Each investor would receive 50.9 cents on the dollar (after tax) after just three years of investing (typical time to develop the property). That would be a little less than a 14% return on investment for the equity investors. However, the promoter, who initially purchased the land, will walk away with an additional 0.523x (after tax) property value. In the end, after taxes, (excluding state and country taxes), a land investor who purchases a plot of land at x, finance 0.4x and provides cash of 0.6x and then goes on to develop it with equity investors participating only in the development side, will stand to make a total of 1.15x + 0.523x which is equal to 1.673x. His original investment was only 0.6x which means he makes a return of 178% in 3 – 4 years. That's approximately a 40% return on his original investment.

The point that you should walk away from is that you get what you work for. If you want to invest in something passively, then the returns are going to reflect that, but, if you invest in something and work at it actively by leveraging the right areas and working the financial assets properly, then you can make supernatural profits and that is the way you build wealth.

The maths would work out differently in different parts of the country because the property prices differ and tax structures will differ as well, and so will the demand for different kinds of property. That will determine the margins you can make for the investment you make.

Chapter 5

Secrets You Haven't Heard About

This chapter is about the things that most beginners have never heard about, and I urge you to tread with caution as you need to check with your lawyers and accountants so that you make the necessary fine tuning that is necessary to fulfill this structure and the profits that can be extracted from it. None of the things that we show you in this book are too far out of the ordinary and none of them are illegal, but you need to check the fine print of the law – as you know who is always hiding in there.

1. The first secret that you have not heard about is the ability to find foreclosed properties that you can pick up – ok, if you've heard of that one, then the next is…

2. Look for distressed properties by advertising for owners who are at the brink of foreclosure and buy them out. It will help them save their credit and it will help you save quite a bit. Anything you can save in terms of purchase price goes a long way. This is a good strategy for those who do not

have a lot of cash but want to get into real estate. What you can do is advertise nationally for those who want to sell their property that is on the brink of foreclosure. If you get it at 0.8x market value, then you only need to come up with a 0.2x down payment and still be within the 0.4% loan rule.

3. Create investment clubs so that you can share the equity of getting into a property when you are still not as liquid as you need to be. Set up a property investment club using a corporation and have everyone pitch in, and then move up the ladder from there.

4. Sell your house to an S Corp which you own, take the cash and invest it in to another property. You can deduct a lot of the home improvements as expenses this way.

5. Aim to sell in the spring and buy in the summer. Average prices tend to fluctuate around these times. Summer typically has lower average prices, while spring generally has higher average prices.

6. Use a real estate agent to buy or sell your home. Tap into them for the best prices and their client list. Strong agents are clued into home buyers and professional property buyers.

7. Always make adjustments and renovations to homes, even if they do not apparently need it.

Fresh paint, fresh renovations, new appliances, and new carpets all make for a significantly higher price during a sale. Be willing to spend a little money on sprucing up the place before inviting buyers.

8. Defer your capital gains tax by purchasing another property within 45 days of the first property's sale. This way, instead of leaking the money into property tax, you can roll it into a larger property and stand to gain a larger profit when you flip that one.

9. The old adage, 'Location, Location, Location', still applies. It's no big secret but it needs to be stressed that you need to see the big picture. Here are five elements of the property that you need to look at:

    a. Location

    b. Access

    c. Zoning

    d. Surrounding

    e. Seller

10. Finally, the secret that you've been waiting for is that you should keep all property that you purchase, whether you are investing in rental property or if it is just a one-off property

investment, always keep it at arm's length.

Chapter 6

Eagle Eye View That Could Give You the Edge

The real estate market has the potential to make you significant profits and, if you look closely at the strategies employed in this book, what you will see is that if you keep the mindset of minimal borrowing, then you will already be one up on the market in general.

How and why?

Well, because most of the real estate market focuses on debt-heavy structures to advance their real estate objectives. This creates a period of inflation during strong money supply times and a deflation of prices during periods of a low money supply.

As you can imagine, the high money supply creates the necessity for banks to liberalize their banking terms and flood the market with low yield debt. A decade ago my bartender told me that he had three homes over a million dollars in debt and it was all being paid by the renters that he had rented the houses out to. Not only had the banks lent him the price of the home where he had zero money down, they tacked on a home equity line for each of the three houses and, in the end, he was levered up 1.3 times the value of his houses. It was an amazing story and pretty endemic of the times. When people can buy houses with cheap money, the price of homes rise rapidly and that, in turn, fuels even more cheap money.

But when the musk stopped, it was the man on the street like this bartender of mine that was left with 1.3 times debt and a deflated market meaning it as actually 1.5 times debt. He declared bankruptcy and lost his homes – including the one he was living in.

That's not the point of this chapter. The point is that when banks are willing to give you more of a loan than what you need, that is the exact time you should look the other way. It means that the property is going to be overvalued.

This is the time you stay away. Spend your time during these periods of easy money, saving yours so that when the time comes, and it most certainly will, that the money supply tightens up, and loans are harder to keep, there will be a flood of properties that you can pick up at better prices.

The fine tuning of this process depends very much on your understanding of the macroeconomic fundamentals of the market you are looking at. If you are in the US, which I assume you are, then you need to look at the economic cycle of the world in general, and the economics of the country as a whole.

There are three areas in particular you need to monitor. You need to look at interest rates in the first cut. In the second cut, you need to look at money supply and ease of credit. In the third cut, you need to look at terms of the debt. If you see highly favorable terms for the first five years and then highly unfavorable terms in the last twenty-five, then you know that, in general, the market is going to be in a lot of trouble in five years. The same banker that is giving you this loan now is giving the same terms to every one of his customers and so are his colleagues – giving it to all their customers. It is a nationwide thing.

My bartender who levered up to 1.3x his properties' value was not a one-off occurrence, it was the norm almost across the country. People were furnishing their homes and buying bigger cars and gadgets as though the money was free. When it all came crashing down, it was the small guy and his family who paid dearly. You cannot afford to make that mistake. You need to time the market entry, the hold-period and then match it along with the times when the money supply is tight and loose. When the money supply is tight, it's when you should buy, because most people would stay out. When the money supply is loose, is when you should unload because people would pay whatever you ask for since their bank is willing to lend them the money.

If you can time the market this way, you will see that they

oscillate in an almost predictable fashion. The timing may not be the same, but that is for you to determine from one case to the next.

The Cycles of the Real Estate Market

The real estate cycle is a function of money supply, consumer sentiment, banking regulation, and the global economy in general. To have a better grasp on it, it is best we lay this out in a sequence that makes sense – from the most effective, to the least. Remember, this is a comparative list so the least doesn't mean that it has no effect on the market, it just means it has the least compared to the others, but it is still a major factor overall.

The list, in descending order, is as follows:

1. Money supply

2. Median income

3. Consumer sentiment

4. Banking regulation

5. Global economy

We already looked at the money supply and so we need to look at the median income. Median income is a function of a number of factors. It has its tentacles in the unemployment rate and in the overall economy of the country (i.e. GDP, growth, etc). The higher the median income, the more demand there is for residential property. The higher the transition from poverty to middle income, the more demand for rental property, and the lower the demand for property purchases.

You need to look at the median income of the city and the county to get an understanding of the kind of property you want to look at if you are interested in residential rental properties. If you want to look at commercial property, then you should speak to the developers who will be able to give you a good idea on the growth rates of the market. This briefing that the agents provide you with is merely the starting point as it gives you a framework to then proceed with verification and research.

Timing the Macro Cycles

It's really of no use to only know that the cycles exist, as you also have to time it so that it works in your favor. Timing it is something that is an instinct that you have to build, but here are a few points that you can use in order to build your timing.

1. The first thing about timing is that it takes

practice to build up the gut feeling to know when to strike. As such, you should not rush it, but keep polishing your investment gut instinct.

2. Never rush for a deal if it is not perfectly baked. There are another million deals out there, so prepare yourself for the next one. Rushing into a deal is the best way to lose money.

3. Every negotiation you have at every stage until the end should be made under the proviso that things are not final. It is only final at the last signing and transfer of funds. Always give yourself an exit.

4. Keep track of the economy and the money supply numbers as well as the discount rate. Get ready to enter when the money dries up, and be ready to put your own money in.

5. Cultivate a strong equity investment club to jump in with you so that you can structure your investments at a moment's notice – it helps with your timing.

With these steps, it makes it easier for you to time your jumps in the macroeconomic cycles.

Chapter 7

Structure Real Estate Investment Companies Like A Pro

Tax Considerations

Remember tax evasion is a crime, tax avoidance is not. That means you cannot run away from taxes that you are otherwise liable for, but you can structure yourself in the smartest way possible to reduce your tax liability. It's not unpatriotic in any way to cut back on the tax exposure. Pay what you owe and not a penny more.

Having said that, there are two reasons you will structure the holdings you have when it comes to anonymity and taxes. The four layers in your structure will give you plenty of anonymity, but it will also give you enough protection against taxes. You don't really want to structure away all your taxes every year, but, at the same time, there are better ways to make returns than skimping on your taxes. So pay what you owe – as little as possible.

All the interest that you pay on a loan for the property is tax deductible. However, if it is a rental property and you are receiving rental from the property that the loan is taken out for and the property is collateralized against that loan, then the interest is not deductible against the rental income.

So, this is how that impacts you. In the example above, if you were receiving $3,000 in rental and paid $2,000 on the loan over 30 years, you were paying almost $300,000 in interest. All of that is tax deductible if the house wasn't collateralized for the loan and, since it is, there is no deduction opportunity here.

However, in the development example, the loan you took had no rental income. You received progress payments over the course of three years. All the interest payments that you made are tax deductible.

So, a good way to structure it if you could swing it with your bank is to postpone principal payments and front-load the interest payments with the understanding that the loan would be paid in full in three years. That way, all the progress payments are tied to expenses and the rest is tax deductible so you have no tax liability for the period.

If you are a C Corp, then your tax liability is also a little different. You will be able to offset capital losses to capital gains – but not other kinds of losses, so you can take operating losses and offset it with capital gains. You can defer the tax by rolling over the gains in the next replacement property.

You need to look at tax as a cost, and the way you reduce your cost is to structure it in the most cost-effective way that you can. You have to balance between capital gains/losses, operating income/loses, depreciation, interest expense, and equity. You also have to worry about double taxation.

For instance, the profit and loss of an LLC flows right through to your personal income tax computation, but the dividend that you receive from shareholding is treated as income – so you land up paying tax twice – once at the corporate level and the other at the personal level. If you keep doing that, it gets pretty expensive after a while. The only way to cut down on this cost is to structure your companies in a way that makes sense for the kinds of investments you want to make. The different structure that can be created for each variation of each individual scenario would be too much for this book, but I do urge you to speak with your accountant and your lawyer to come to some kind of a consensus on how to package the whole thing together so that you can reduce your tax liability significantly.

A good tax strategy would be to look at Real Estate Investment Trusts, and we'll look at that in another book. That is a whole other topic that you will definitely find very interesting and you could potentially make money as an issuer or as an investor.

To keep it simple here, keep these few time-tested strategies that you can use, to look for areas to trim the tax bill:

1. Expense the interest whenever possible.

2. Roll over the profits of the property into a new property.

3. Mortgage one property to buy another property for cash – so that you can expense the interest costs.

Offshore Company Set-Up

Offshore companies have little advantage when it comes to structuring the cost and taxes of a real estate investment company. Foreign entities must continue to pay taxes on income and on vehicles that can also be used by domestic entities, but offshore company set-ups have a significant benefit in other areas. The way you should look at it is to have one layer that maximizes the flow through of cash, but stops short excess liability within the entity. The second layer should be to minimize costs to the shareholder and, by that, I mean specifically the taxes that are paid with profits.

Remember that cash does not mean the same thing as profit. It is possible for you to show a profit on the books but, at the same time, not have the cash to settle your taxes – the tax authority is the last body on earth you want to short-change or delay a payment to. At the same time, you want to minimize this cost as much as possible through various means of structuring. You need to balance cash flow considerations with income considerations.

However, then there is the third layer and that is the blanket anonymity. Being anonymous is not about being a crook. It's not just crooks who are trying to hide from the law, and that's not what you are trying to do when you stand behind the veil of a company.

It is so that you and your family are protected from overzealous litigants for whatever dispute may arise from one or more of your properties. It is also a way to ring-fence the losses of one company to remain within that company and not flow through to the ultimate shareholder(s).

An offshore company set up does three things:

1. It is typically anonymous and has no legal relationship with the shareholders and the ultimate owners of the funds.

2. It is typically beyond the reach of county, state

and federal authorities and cannot clamp down on the assets that are in its name unless there is a criminal violation. Even then, it's only the property that can be affected and if the cash has already been moved to the offshore company's foreign accounts, those assets are beyond reach for almost anyone. Do keep in mind that they are not beyond the reach of the US government if those funds are part of an organized crime or if there are unpaid taxes on it.

3. It is particularly good at shielding your true wealth and that plays in nicely with your efforts in succession planning.

If you exceed $10 million in holdings, it is advisable that you start to gradually move that offshore but leave it denominated in US dollars. A really good way to do that these days is to convert the cash to cryptocurrency and move that out of the country to a destination of your choice, and then convert it back to USD at your destination, and deposit it into a bank account under this offshore company. That offshore company should be held in trust. That is a simple structure and it is highly unlikely anyone (except the US government) can trace those assets back to you.

When you structure your real estate investments, it will inevitably be an organic affair. You couldn't possibly set up all the entities in a complicated web from the start. It will cost you a lot of money and it will be extremely inefficient. Corporate and investment structures serve the function, and it cannot be the other way around. You have to set the structure of your investment vehicles in a way that is attuned and appropriate to the ecosystem you operate in and in the assets that you invest in. If you solely purchased rental properties in one state, then your structure would be a lot simpler because it would only have to take into consideration the statutory costs of one jurisdiction, the tax burden of the county, state and federal jurisdictions; and the regulations of the same three. That makes everything simple and you can tie them off with lower costs because of efficiencies in operational scale.

This set-up gets more complex and more involved the moment you step out into different states. Everything from company registration and annual fees, all the way to the way easements are handled, will change across different jurisdictions. You need to think about these issues when you structure your set-up, but the problem is that the best way to do this is with experience. No book can ever tell you all the possible differences and nuances that could possibly be listed out. Structuring is like Kung-Fu. You need to be able to roll with the purchases and be agile on your feet and, just like with Kung-Fu, you need to be able to focus on the objective that matters, and in property, there are two –asset protection and cost-effectiveness.

Asset protection includes all the efforts that keep it away

from prying eyes and protects it from spillover risks of other properties. Cost-effectiveness is more about taking advantage of the tax treatment of certain structures and reaping the higher profits from that.

As long as you keep your focus on these factors, then you will have no problem maneuvering the landscape and getting the most efficient corporate structure. You already have the basics. If you look at the four-tiered structure in Chapter 3, that is your starting point. From there on, you can vary the structure in ways that suit the situation and the purpose.

You need three professionals in your team at all times. You need a lawyer who understands real estate. You need an accountant that understands state and federal taxes, and you need an administration person who can put documents together and prepare all the paperwork you need in short order – someone who is like a short order cook in a diner.

Your job in this set-up will be to go out and look for opportunities. These three people will know your entire structure all the way up to the holding level company in the United States, but they will not know anything about your offshore company. Only you should know about that.

Chapter 8

Ways to Cut Losses and Let Profits Ride

This chapter should come a little earlier in the book because the tone of the book has been one that has been increasing in its detail and sophistication, and this topic seems to be something that is a little more basic.

The reason it is back here is so you can look at losses in a way that is outside your main focus. You shouldn't really be thinking about losses in such detail early in the game, but you should still want to mitigate them. Here is the hierarchy of how you deal with losses:

1. Focus on deals that are superior, even if they cost a little more. It is easier to cover a shortfall on a good deal than to salvage a bad one.

2. Never fall in love with a piece of property. If it starts to lose money, cut the losses early.

3. Never hold the property beyond the macroeconomic cycle that you predict. If you don't exit at the apex, that's ok, it is never

possible to liquidate assets at the apex of market prices. As long as you made superior profit, that's good. Just learn from this transaction so that you can improve on the next transaction.

4. Anonymity has different levels of opacity. At the lowest level, it is completely transparent and, as you ascend in the structure, it gets decreasingly so until the final offshore or holding company is totally anonymous as far as shareholding and valuations are concerned.

In all the structures that you end up using, you have seen that we repeatedly stress that the structure must be one that values cost reduction and asset protection. We looked at taxes earlier, and how you need to find ways to go about reducing that cost, but there is another cost that we do not really classify or think about as a cost. That is the cost of loss.

Just as profits have a cost, losses have a cost too. It costs money to unwind relationships, and it costs money to end contracts and terminate matters. It even costs money to liquidate properties. Someone or something needs to be responsible for these costs and it is typically the owner of the property.

This is the main reason you ring-fence all your properties into separate entities. This is also the reason that you keep a certain level of cash and liquid assets in the company so that you can cover predictable costs and unpredictable costs that arise over the course of the ownership.

The most important reason is that those costs should be kept within the universe of that property and not be allowed to spill over. Spilling over has the effect of dominoes. If all your properties are at a specific age in your portfolio, then they have a certain risk sensitivity and profile. If they are burdened by cash requirements from an overflow of losses, then the failure could spread from one property to the next, and then to the next, until your entire portfolio faces ruin like a ship that springs a leak in the hull but it is not compartmentalized, and the flooding spreads from one compartment to the next until the entire ship is breached and sinks. For the same reason, ships have compartments to seal off so that the rest of the ship can continue floating. You too have to treat each property as an individual compartment. The moment it becomes problematic, you need to cut your losses and liquidate that position.

In most cases, I would tell you to lose as much money as you put into it, and not a penny more. There are some strategies that use debt for this. They say that if you use high levels of debt and the property goes under, then the entity can just write it off and let the bank take the hit. Don't do that because it may work in the short-term, but what you are trying to build alongside your property business is a good relationship with the bank. You must be able to say your name, and banks line up to provide the credit you need when you need it. If you make it a habit of cutting losses and leaving the bank to hold your losses, eventually the credit market will dry up for you and that will severely impact your rates of return and your ability to grow.

Keeping this in mind, you will have a better understanding of the reason behind the larger down payment we advocated earlier in the book. The larger the down payment, the lower the return on investment, and the lower the risk you face in terms of unanticipated losses ruining the entire investment. The debt levels that were chosen can be altered once you get a good grip on the risk of the investment and the down payment. The experience you will gain in time is to vary the debt to equity ratios that you employ in each type of real estate investment.

Here is a strategy that I would like you to consider. You have an office building that you plan on buying and it has 100 tenants. No single tenant has more than 3% of the total office space rented from you and contributes no more than 3% of your monthly rental cash flow. None of them have missed a payment in five years. Let's call your monthly rental X. Your operating expenses are 0.11x and the building is priced at 200x (market value). At 4.5% interest, the maximum loan you can take for this building is exactly 200x and your monthly payments for a 30 year fixed rate loan is 0.8x. It is predicted that the asset will be worth 4 times its present market value in 15 years.

The best way to structure this would be to have two separate loans. The first loan is for 30% of the value of the asset. For this loan, you provide the building as collateral. The interest from this is not tax deductible. With the second loan, you have a management company that takes a loan out for 70% of the purchase price and that is secured by the cash flow of the tenants. Collateralizing the building obviates the interest payments as use in tax calculations, but collateralizing cash flows does not. Now, you can deduct the interest payments from the second loan that collateralized the cash flows while keeping the building out of the equation. The tax saving is the kind of thing that we are talking about. There is nothing illegal about it, nor is it immoral. It is just smart and it is not something that you can find in textbooks, but the smart money will know how to structure to reduce costs as much as possible.

Look at everything in terms of cost, value and risk. Reduce your cost, increase your value and erect all mechanisms to isolate and mitigate risk. That's the name of the game when it comes to real estate investing. It really is three-dimensional chess and, in time, you will be rewarded for your efforts.

Coming back to cutting losses.

Here are three things that you have to do when you plan

for the purchase of the property. This is in addition to all the things that we talked about before, but this one is specifically about cutting your losses and you should think of this by the time you close on the deal.

1. List all the costs of winding up at every stage of the investment. You should already have a cash flow that projects out to the end of the investment horizon and, at the bottom line, you should calculate ahead of time the cost of liquidating at that point in time. You can do this in six-month intervals.

2. Have an investment fund that is fairly liquid, giving you a return that matches the rate of inflation and keep this as the emergency funds for assets that may have a problem. Don't touch this unless absolutely necessary.

3. Build multiple companies with strong credit ratings so that you can eventually move away from giving personal guarantees for the loans. The moment you provide a personal guarantee, all the structuring that you do to protect the assets become diluted. Your personal guarantee means that in the event of a loss, or an unavoidable situation, you and your other assets come into the equation.

With these three steps, what you are during is that in the

event the tripwire for loss is triggered, you can instantly make moves to cut the losses and get out with at least a little equity left, or with at least no need to cover additional losses. Never let losses run in the hope that things will turn around.

The next thing that you need to do when it comes to cutting losses is to extract a guarantee from the seller that they will provide a warranty for the critical items in the building for at least five years after the sale. For instance, if the equipment is not as they said it would be over the next five years, you are not saddled with the cost of rectifying it. Bringing this cost upfront, by having to pay a slightly higher premium on the purchase price, will strengthen the structure and keep you from unintended losses.

Predictability is worth the premium, unpredictability is not worth the risk. There are two kinds of risk that you should understand - acceptable risk and unacceptable risk. Acceptable risk is a function of the normal course of life. If you have the staying power to overcome it, you can ride it out and come out clear on the other side with the profit that you deserve for holding on to the situation. Then there is unacceptable risk. This risk is the kind that you shouldn't take on because no matter how long you hold on to it, it is not going to change.

Think of it this way - flooding is an acceptable risk. You can mitigate it by building a wall, you can take out flood insurance and you can make changes to the property, but changing sea levels that threaten to submerge the entire area is not an acceptable risk. The reason you want to keep this in your mind is because wealth is not made by running away from risk, it is made by finding ingenious ways of mitigating it. The point that the risk cannot be mitigated is the point that you need to cut your losses. The more you do your homework before taking possession, the less unmanageable risk situations you will be faced with. If you find yourself in that position, it is always best to seal off and jettison a losing venture than to infect the other assets.

Risk can be foreseen and you may be in a unique situation to mitigate a particular risk if you can see ahead. That is the core of wealth-building ventures. Real estate gives you these opportunities because it has different dimensions that you can play with to take advantage of. You just have to make the decision that there is no reason you should lose money because of a mistake.

The best way to minimize your loss is to do your homework and to do it quick. Opportunities come quick and vanish fast. You can't rush into them because that's the best way to make errors in judgment, so, how do you get to the finish line ahead if you take so much time to make a decision?

Smart investors have a well-defined profile of what they will and what they will not invest in. You should have an investment criteria that you build from the beginning so that you specialize in one area and do not stray from that.

The longer you do this, the faster your response time gets without having to rush.

Conclusion

There is a lot that we have covered in a short book. It is designed to get you up to speed in an area that you have no experience in, and it is designed to mold your mindset to think as a real estate investor.

The primary frame of mind that you should have is the profit potential, and if you are just investing in property to keep the purchasing power of the dollar the same from one year to the next, or if you are looking to make your money to work for you so that your asset can create an income without eroding the bulk that you have saved up. The third reason we invest in real estate could be that we want to build wealth. These are three broad frames of mind. All three have different risk and return profiles, and all three have different mindsets to manage.

In the first, your choice of properties will be limited to stable rental properties, even commercial rental properties, to keep your income predictable. In the second situation, the types of investments could be high-end single-family homes and, in the third situation, you could find yourself investing in land and developing them.

The thing that changes is the risk profile and the effort that needs to be put in. The one with the least amount of effort and least amount of risk gives you the least amount of return. The one with the most amount of effort and risk gives you the most return.

You have to be smart about real estate investments and you need to be able to structure them to be able to extract the profits as efficiently as possible. It takes a lot of homework and it takes man hours to do it. You would be best served by having a small amount of staff to help you with the repetitive task, and then outsource the functions that require specializations. Take, for instance, inspectors and valuers do not need to be in your employ, you can outsource them if and when you need their services.

In the meantime, you need to hone up on your knowledge and your familiarity with different regulations, different jurisdictions, the types of properties and the way the markets work.

The stories you see on TV do not apply to the way property investment really works. Most of the investment is planned out ahead of time and the risk and its effects are considered before they are taken on. The ones that absolutely cannot be absorbed are insured out to professional insurers and the cost is taken into account before the first penny is paid towards the investment.

Finally, I know that you are very likely to be a person trying to start up a real estate business from home, and that is fine; in fact, it is to be commended. It's ok to work from home, but it's not okay to treat this as a home business or a cottage industry. You need to treat real estate investments as a serious business with serious consequences and ramifications to each decision and each move. You need to do whatever it takes to put yourself into that frame of mind. There is a reason why working from home for some people may not be ideal because they can't get to transition from their home duties and into the mindset of a business owner. It's one thing if you are making jam or soup in your kitchen and have a small website selling it, but it is a whole different thing when you are planning to develop a piece of land.

Do whatever it takes to get you into the frame of mind that allows you to see the business you are in clearly, and see what you have to do in a way that advances your goals rather than diminishes them. Real estate investing can be the doorway to financial security, financial freedom and even wealth-building, but it all starts with how much of your mind you want to invest.

Good luck.

Thank You!

Before you go, we would like to thank you for purchasing a copy of our book. Out of the dozens of books you could have picked over ours, you decided to go with this one and for that we are very grateful.

We hope you enjoyed reading it as much as we enjoyed writing it! We hope you found it very informative.

We would like to ask you for a small favor. <u>Could you please take a moment to leave a review for this book on Amazon?</u>

Your feedback will help us continue to write more books and release new content in the future!

More Books By

Money Grind Academy

- <u>Real Estate Investing: What Every New Investor Needs to Know About Investing in Real Estate</u>

www.ingramcontent.com/pod-product-compliance
Lightning Source LLC
Chambersburg PA
CBHW020444220526
45464CB00002B/847